SKYSCRAPERS

MAN-MADE WONDERS

Jason Cooper

Rourke Enterprises, Inc.
Vero Beach, Florida 32964

PHOTO CREDITS

© Lynn M. Stone: cover, title page, pages 4, 8, 10, 12-13, 15, 17, 18;
© Frank Balthis: page 7; © Arthur Swoger: page 21

LIBRARY OF CONGRESS
Library of Congress Cataloging-in-Publication Data
Cooper, Jason, 1942-
   Skyscrapers / by Jason Cooper.
   p. cm. — (Man made wonders)
   Includes bibliographical references and index.
   Summary: Discusses the nature, history, and building of
skyscrapers.
   ISBN 0-86592-637-9
   1. Skyscrapers—United States—Juvenile literature.
[1. Skyscrapers.]
I. Title. II. Series.
NA6232.C66 1991
720.'483—dc20   91-10951
                  CIP
                  AC

TABLE OF CONTENTS

SKYSCRAPERS

Skyscrapers are the world's tallest buildings. Stand at the base of one of these giants and look up. On clear days, the skyscraper's top seems to scrape the sky. When clouds are low, skyscraper tops vanish like tall mountains in mist.

The first skyscraper stood just ten **stories,** or floors, tall. Today some of these wonders of steel, glass, and concrete have over 100 stories!

Skyscraper peaks reach for the sun

THE FIRST SKYSCRAPER

Buildings with more than one story have been around for a long time. But the idea that a building could tower above the ground is new.

The first skyscraper was the Home Insurance Building in Chicago. Built in 1884-1885, it was torn down in 1931.

The Home Insurance Building was the first tall building to be built on a steel frame. The use of steel frames made much taller skyscrapers possible. Today's modern skyscrapers are still framed in steel.

Steel-frame skyscrapers crowd the Seattle skyline

WHY SKYSCRAPERS?

True skyscrapers are found in many big cities. Land is scarce in the central part of big cities, and it is expensive.

What, then, does a company do when it needs a huge building in the center of downtown? It builds upward instead of outward.

By building a skyscraper, a company does not need much land. Tall buildings also save money in building materials.

Skyscrapers provide space for offices, restaurants, stores, apartments, and hotel rooms.

Modern, big cities, like Sydney, Australia, build upward

BUILDING SKYSCRAPERS DOWN

A skyscraper is something like a giraffe's neck. It is long and tall, and it is supported by a skeleton and strong "legs."

A skyscraper's skeleton though is steel, not bone. Its legs are buried tons of concrete and steel.

In building skyscrapers, what goes up must first go down. The supports under a skyscraper are set deep into the ground until they hit solid rock. Once the skyscraper's "legs" are in place, the building itself begins to rise.

John Hancock Center in Chicago rises 1,127 feet from a buried bed of supports

The Chicago skyline of modern skyscrapers, including Sears Tower (left), the world's tallest

BUILDING SKYSCRAPERS UP

The skeleton of a skyscraper is a frame of steel pieces. Many huge machines called **cranes** are used to lift the steel into place.

Windows, floors, and side sections are added, story by story. The weight of the building is supported by the rock, concrete, and steel underneath the skyscraper. As heavy as the building is, it is much lighter than if it had been built of solid brick or stone.

Cranes add another floor to a skyscraper

CHICAGO: CITY OF SKYSCRAPERS

Until William LeBaron Jenney designed Chicago's first steel-frame skyscraper, big buildings were made of stone and brick.

Jenney's plan became the model for dozens of skyscrapers that followed. And Chicago became known for its skyscrapers.

Chicago is still the city of skyscrapers. Seven of the world's twenty-one tallest buildings—and three of the tallest five—are in Chicago.

Other major skyscrapers are in New York City, Los Angeles, Houston, Seattle, Dallas, Toronto, and Singapore.

Skyscrapers along Chicago's Lake Michigan shoreline

THE SEARS TOWER

The world's tallest building is the Sears Tower in Chicago. Sears Tower rises 1,454 feet from sidewalk to roof. It has 110 stories.

Built by Sears, Roebuck, and Company, the Tower took three years to complete. It opened in September, 1973.

Nearly 76,000 tons of steel and 1,500 miles of electric lines were used in the Tower.

Like other skyscrapers, Sears Tower will sway slightly in hard winds.

At 1,454 feet, Sears Tower is the world's tallest building

FAMOUS SKYSCRAPERS

One of the world's most famous buildings is the Empire State Building in New York City. When it opened in 1931, it was the world's tallest building—102 stories and 1,250 feet high.

The Empire State Building remained the world's tallest building until 1972. It now ranks third, behind Sears Tower and New York's World Trade Center.

Chicago's Amoco Building (1,136 feet) and John Hancock Center (1,127 feet) rank fourth and fifth.

Empire State Building (left) and World Trade Center (right) in New York City

SKYSCRAPERS OF TOMORROW

Skyscrapers will continue to rise along the **skylines** of big cities. As old office buildings are torn down, dazzling skyscrapers take their places.

How tall can a skyscraper be? Today's skyscrapers already stand taller than four football fields set end to end. It is likely that some skyscrapers of the future will be even taller.

Architects have already drawn plans for a new "World's Tallest Building." If it is built, it will be 125 stories high. And it will be in Chicago, the city of skyscrapers.

Glossary

architect (ARK uh tekt) — someone who designs buildings, bridges

crane (KRAYN) — a machine with a long, swinging arm for lifting heavy weights

skyline (SKI line) — an outline of a city's buildings against the sky

story (STOR ee) — one floor of a building

INDEX